The Wait:
Navigating Spiritually
Through COVID-19

21 Days of Inspiration

by

Joel Floyd, PhD

Praise for _The Wait: Navigating Spiritually Through COVID-19_

Dr. Joel Floyd hit the mark with **_The Wait: Navigating Spiritually through COVID-19_**. He masterfully compares this ambiguous pandemic season to a waiting room and encourages readers to look beyond the many delays and dig deeper to realize that there is true purpose in the wait. In a time of immense uncertainty, Dr. Floyd reminds readers of certain truths; the faithfulness of God and the power of the spoken word.

The daily devotions are filled with hope, encouragement and spiritual nourishment.   I highly recommend this book for those who are seeking guidance and inspiration during this season of life!

Rainbow Huff – Author of 31 Devotions for The Empowered Woman

Nashville, TN

"In the waiting room, God has given you the ability to find your peace as though you were in the eye of a very powerful hurricane! I encourage you to find your peace and ride with it until the COVID19 storm subsides (Day 8)." Dr. Floyd, Dr. Floyd……The Wait: Navigating Spiritually Through COVID 19 is **Amazing, Captivating, and Splendid.** Dr. Joel Floyd is an astonishing, divine, and remarkable teacher of inspiration using the **Words of Gods waiting room and**

the real life of the challenging, difficult, and uncertain times of COVID 19. I loved and enjoyed reading the 21 days of Inspiration and I adore the author as well. Beyond doubt I would recommend The Wait: Navigating Spiritually through COVID 19. Dr. Floyd incorporated the scriptures into the book to remind the readers that God has his all-powerful hands in this pot. Amen

SAAKA1908, BS, MS

Gulfport, MS

TABLE OF CONTENTS

Introduction

C haos fills the world. Tomorrow is uncertain. What once was is no longer. Joblessness, homelessness, and loneliness have become a tragic reality. The doors of many churches across the globe have been closed, creating deep feelings of hopelessness in the minds of many. Panic, fear, and the killer coronavirus disease known as COVID-19 have all become commonplace, and we have been forced to sit in the waiting room.

This book is not a story of my life or some mysterious finding. There are no conspiracy theories concerning our current and novel global pandemic. Rather, this book is a short 21-day devotional designed to inspire you and to give you a sense of hope while you are journeying through the waiting room of great and abrupt uncertainty. Unfortunately, this waiting room is abundantly filled with many twists and turns, some more tragic than others, and there is clearly an emergency. We all feel it. No one person is exempt: We're all waiting to see what the doctor has to say.

There are many recurring questions: What about tomorrow? What is next? How do I embrace this new normal? How do I survive? Do I live? Do I die? Do I sink or do I swim? Each of these questions is critically valid, and while I certainly do not profess to know it all, if we're to survive, it is imperative, I believe, that we obtain spiritual strategies while in the waiting room.

It is my hope that each waking day, you allow any one of these daily devotions to speak to your heart and give you a deeper sense of hope, despite the conditions of your present and future waiting room experiences. I believe it is in the quiet, early, and fleeting moments of the day that we feel and sense God's heartbeat.

Come with me. Together, let's be inspired and survive together.

Author's Note

Before you journey with me over the next 21 days, I'd like you to consider these things: Despite the destruction that the abrupt and unforeseen monster COVID-19 has superimposed upon humanity globally, we have all been given a vision and/or a purpose for living. Your cultural, socioeconomic, and racial backgrounds do not impact the fact that God has created a special role for you to fulfill in the universe. I believe that the waiting room of COVID-19 is challenging you and me to revisit and refine our vision or life purposes.

Before the genesis of COVID-19, many of us were so immersed in trying to survive every day that, perhaps, our God-given vision had become somewhat cloudy. Perhaps, our comfort zones were just enough to pretend that we were fulfilling our highest calling. Nonetheless, I believe that the waiting room experience of COVID-19 is giving us the opportunity to obtain new clarity concerning our vision, and soon we will receive the full manifestation of every God-given dream that has been planted in our hearts. More than this, the waiting room of COVID-19 is challenging us to self-reflect. We must be willing to enter into a deeper level of both practical and spiritual introspection. Now is the time to dig deep into our inner selves and allow God to reveal the changes we need to make critical to fulfilling our greatest God-given potential.

Finally, I believe that the waiting room of COVID-19, though heartbreaking for many, is preparing each of us for something greater that has yet to be revealed. The slowdown that we are currently experiencing has been orchestrated by God, the Creator, giving us the opportunity to re-connect with our higher power (God) on both an authentic and personal level. The waiting room of COVID-19 is more than what we see. This waiting room is a spiritual phenom-enon, so let's get excited about what God has for each of us as we wait.

DAY 1:

FRIDAY

"Trust in the Lord with all your heart, and do not lean to your own understanding."

Proverbs 3: 5

F riday is probably one of the most exciting days for many in the United States of America. Friday ends the workweek. Pre- COVID Friday was the realization that you made it to the finish line. Despite all the challenges and abrupt and unforeseen troubles that may have come with the workweek, there was something uniquely endearing about Friday. For many, the weekend means rest and relaxation, as well as family and/or a mini-vacation time.

While in our current waiting room, Friday has come again, but for many, there is no work to be freed from and no abrupt plans to fulfill, but can you maintain the same feeling of excitement that you previously felt before COVID-19? Can you still trust God and believe that everything is going to be just fine?

As a young boy growing up in a Pentecostal church I sang a song entitled, "I've Got a Feeling (Everything's going to be alright)." This was probably one of my all-time favorite Gospel songs. The words of this song felt so positive. The song gave me the assurance that I, along with my church family, had nothing to worry about. Recurring visions of victory refreshed my mental states as the song was sung. Simply, God was going to take care of us. I still believe this today. Do you?

Say with me: Everyday is a Friday, for I trust in the name of the Lord.

DAY 2:

MOVE

"Then suddenly a woman who had been suffering from hemorrhages for twelve years came up behind him and touched the fringe of [Jesus'] cloak for she said to herself, if I only touch his cloak, I will be made well."

Matthew 9: 20-21

In one of the synoptic Gospels, there was a woman who was diagnosed with an incurable disease, a very bad blood condition, and there was no such understanding as with modern medicine as we know it today. According to the biblical account, the woman, whose name is not mentioned, exhausted all of her resources hoping to obtain a cure for her condition.

All hope was not lost!

The woman had heard of a man by the name of Jesus, a healer who had been travelling through the land, curing people of various diseases. Something in the woman's psyche leaped, causing her to make a move despite her physical condition. She declared to herself, "If I can just reach the presence of Jesus, I know that I will be completely healed."

While in the waiting room, you, too, may be facing sickness or disease or perhaps, your darkness is dealing with a financial crisis, a current loss of employment, a denial of unemployment, feelings of family and/or government let-down, or you may be asking God, "Why? Why is this happening to me? Why do bad things happen to good people? Why, God, why me?"

I don't know the background of the woman with the blood disease, but I admire her for her willingness to move forward in faith until she reached the feet of Jesus. Oftentimes, we are so blinded by an unfavorable waiting room experience that we refuse to move. It's easier to sit back and complain, call a friend, and have a pity party.

I encourage you to get up and move. The waiting room of COVID-19 is not your final destination. You will be surprised the miracles that will erupt in your life when you get to moving despite the situation.

Just move!

Say with me: I am moving past every insurmountable circumstance, and as a result of my movement, I will experience miracles and blessings that I have not begun to imagine.

DAY 3:

DANCE

"Let [us] praise the name of the Lord with dancing."

Psalm 149: 3

The conditions of life, whether good or bad, abrupt or planned are all inevitable. It is no secret that no one—believers or non-believers—can control the uncertainties of tomorrow. During my short time on earth, I've learned that those who succeed at accomplishing a goal were able to dance even when the challenges of life did not warrant a dance. I have learned that I may not be able to control the condition, but I can control myself.

Although I am not a dancer at all, I consider dancing a type of rejoicing. Have you ever danced around the house, in your car, with friends, at a concert, or wherever? How did your dance make you feel?

I've read countless reports revealing how dancing reduces stress, counters depression, and improves one's cardiovascular health to a degree. Oh, what a gift, the gift of dance, that God has given to us all! The good news is (just like me) you don't have to be good dancer; all you need to do is move in a spirit of rejoice-edness.

Our dance is an indicator that we are victorious, and we will maintain victory even in the waiting room, despite whatever the final outcome may be.

I hope you dance!

Say with me: I dance unto you, Oh God, for in my dance, I experience great victory over the things I cannot control.

DAY 4:

WAIT

"I believe that I shall look upon the goodness of the Lord in the Land of the living! Wait for the Lord; be strong, and let your heart take courage; wait for the Lord!"

Psalm 27:13-14

In today's society, modern advances in technology have given humanity across the globe something I call Q.A. (Quick Access). At the touch of a button, we discover and obtain the information we request in seconds. Technology and data science have created breakthroughs for corporations to access and use data to their advantage without thinking twice. Furthermore, the brains of millions of millennials are bombarded by technology and the world of social media. In addition, without certain technologies, some companies cannot function. Ultimately, to wait on anything has become a distant memory. No one wants to wait! We have to have it—whatever our "it" is—and it must be now.

I recall a biblical character, a woman whose name is Hannah. The story reveals that Hannah was both a woman of prayer and a faithful woman, who visited the house of the Lord annually. She was filled with faith and worshiped God daily. Despite all of this, Hannah was a barren woman. She could not have a child. It appeared that Hannah did all of the right things in a religious or spiritual sense, but why would Hanna's God shut her womb? Hannah's story is no different from what we are currently facing today. There are many of us who have lived a good life and a life dedicated to service, and then, all of a sudden, it feels as though the rug of destiny, the rug of purpose, and the rug of love from the Creator have been snatched from under our feet.

While in Hanna's uncontrolled waiting room of being a barren woman, she decided to wait on her God. She cried out. She worshiped while she waited. She refused to give up. The story later informs that Hanna eventually conceived and gave birth to a baby boy and named him Samuel. Hannah's waiting room experiences was surely a test of faith and patience, but she waited until she received her answer.

Say with me: There's a blessing in the wait.

DAY 5:

POWER

"For God has not given us a spirit of fear but of power and love and of self-control."

2 Timothy 2: 17

Five years ago, I decided to pursue a doctoral degree in educational leadership. As a current business owner of an English language school for adult learners, it made sense to pursue the Ph.D. I had gained lots of experience as a nascent business leader, and the doctorate in leadership, I believed, would guide my administrative role from a theoretical standpoint.

My business coach, an older generation Caucasian gentleman said to me, "Surely, you cannot purse a Ph.D. in all seriousness and run a business full-time. You have to be nuts. If I were you, I would focus solely on my business and pursue that doctorate later on down the line." While I listened to his advice in a very attentive manner, my heart was set on returning to school to pursue my highest and final degree.

While writing my dissertation, I reached my breaking point. I wanted to quit. My research topic was not that popular, and I was having major difficulty finding previous studies related to it. One day, I looked out of my office window and said to myself, "I should not have done this. I should have listened to my business coach. I really can't do this. It's just too much, and I don't have the time." I began to have a pity party, and tears of sadness began to cover my face.

Later, I began to feel a sense of great resilience due to the power of prayer. My inner spirit encouraged me with these words: "You can do this—dig deeper." At that very moment, I commanded my inner power to be my guide, and my perspective quickly changed. What seemed insurmountable concerning my research had quickly become a manageable task. My inner power gave me the ability to pull myself together, and eventually finish that difficult portion a few days later.

Survival in the waiting room means tapping into and staying connected to your inner power source. The good news is we all have power. It comes from above.

Say with me: My God-given power secures me and gives me victory over every obstacle.

DAY 6:

WHAT IF

"Do you want to be made well?"

John 5: 6

As a young boy growing up, I'd always wonder what older folk meant when they described certain life events as being a blessing in disguise, and I've lived long enough now to understand that blessings don't always come in the way that we, as humans, think they should.

John's gospel records the life of a man, who was sick for thirty-eight years. The text reveals that the man struggled with an infirmity, but does not state what the specific infirmity or sickness was. As I revisited the biblical narrative of the man's unfavorable condition, I learned that he likely could not walk, for he informed the great healer of the day, Jesus, that whenever the water was troubled by an angel at the pool side of Bethesda, many people were healed of whatever sickness or disease they had. All they had to do was step into the moving water. Unfortunately, he had no help getting to the water.

I can only imagine the way this man must have felt-deep feelings of being left behind, counted out, depressed, lonely, and isolated. What a waiting room of utter despair! Think about the many times when you waited to experience something great to manifest in your own life, while it appeared that everyone else around you was already obtaining the very thing you desired.

Jesus eventually showed up and healed the man of his disease even though the man gave Jesus several reasons why he had not been healed. While the story does not reveal why people near the man did not help him get to the healing water, could it be that Jesus wanted to reveal his divine healing power directly to the man? Maybe you're feeling perplexed in the waiting room. I have good news for you. Open your heart. What if Jesus has allowed you to experience an unfortunate waiting room experience because he wants to have a one-to-one encounter with you, too?

Say with me: My God-sized "what if" is about to become a mind-blowing reality.

DAY 7:

STAND

"Don't be afraid. Stand firm and watch [God's]
work of salvation for you today."

Exodus 14: 13

For many, the waiting room can be a terrifying experience. Fear of the unknown is common to us all. We
are not wired to expect the unexpected, especially when life
and culture are guided by our plans and desires.

I recall three radical biblical characters commonly
known as the Hebrew boys. These boys were committed to
their faith. They refused to put any other gods before their
God, the God of Israel. Their refusal to bow down to the

king's golden image got them in lots of trouble, and they were sentenced into the king's fire and furnace. We can definitely agree that these young boys' hearts were consumed with fear, but they refused to abandon their God. The Hebrew boys were willing to stand firm in their belief. They believed that their God would deliver them. Their waiting room experience was one of terror. Can you imagine being severely punished over your refusal to believe in another person's god? Can you imagine being thrown into a pit of fire? What an ineffable punishment!

Despite the waiting room experience you've been given, never forget that the God of your life is forever present.

Say with me: I will never be consumed by the fires of this life for God is with me always.

DAY 8:

PEACE

"I have told you these things, so that in me you may have peace. In this world you will have trouble. But take heart! I have overcome the world."

John 16: 33

Growing up in Florida, the Sunshine State, weather conditions were not always that sunny. The words "Hurricane Season" are quite familiar to most Floridians. Hurricanes are monster storms and can be quite terrifying. They come with an unstoppable fury and in various categories. A Category 5 is the most destructive hurricane, having the ability to demolish anything in its path.

Despite the terror that comes with hurricane type behavior, there is something I love about these monster storms. For example, the eye wall of every hurricane is the area of calmness surrounded by destructive winds. More than that, planes are flown through the eye to collect critical data concerning the storm's path. What a mystery! How is it that a storm so powerful can yet be so peaceful?

In the waiting room, God has given you the ability to find your peace as though you were in the eye of a very powerful hurricane! I encourage you to find your peace and ride with it until the COVID-19 storm subsides.

Say with me: Even in the midst of chaos, God's peace consumes my soul.

DAY 9:

FAITH

"For [it is a good thing] to walk by faith and not by sight."

2 Corinthians 5: 7

In the year 2012, I decided it was time for me to start my own business. I had no money. I had no rich parents to help me. I had no bank loan. I had nothing but the $500 that I had managed to save from a previous job. People around me and even family members cautioned me that without sufficient funding, there would be no way to start a school. It would be impossible to rent out a space and pay someone to assist me with my dream business.

My vision was so great, despite all of the red flags. How was it that I could start a business without enough revenue? Now, I am certainly not saying that we should not be prepared when entering into a new venture, but there are critical times in our life when we must step out of our comfort zones and believe even when we can't see clearly. That's faith! Faith is having full confidence that the outcome is going to work in your favor. My faith produced an unwavering assurance that having my own school was more than a thought; it would become a reality. Today, I am running a successful adult English language institution, which has provided countless adults the ability to improve their lives in the USA by mastering the English language.

Oftentimes, we have nothing to work with while in the waiting room. We don't have the knowledge or the resources to sustain. It feels as though our answer depends on the knowledge or the opinion of others. A best response, however, to your waiting room experience is to let faith lead the way, for with faith comes hope, and with hope comes clarity, and with clarity comes a peace of mind, and with a peace of mind comes the manifestation of the very thing that you were believing in God for, even in the waiting room.

Say with me: I am learning to walk by faith and not by sight. I choose to faith my life forward.

DAY 10:

STILL

"Be still, and know that I am God!"

Psalm 46:10

Our inability to be still is evidenced in our human DNA. As humans, we were created with purpose and lots of it. Our minds are constantly moving, and there is a persistent need to know. We are on a quest, seeking understanding, but what happens when we are suddenly no longer in control and are challenged to truly live life one day at a time? During this current COVID-19 crisis, many of us had plans and by now you've probably thought, "I would have been doing this or I should have been doing that." This type of waiting room experience feels absolutely foreign, and it's easier to enter panic mode than to sit back and wait on God.

Mark's gospel records a very dangerous windstorm. Jesus, accompanied by his disciples, was on a big boat travelling alongside other boats. The storm's winds were so treacherous that the boat looked as if it were going to sink. Fear consumed the disciples' minds. They were terrified. They instantly entered a waiting room of pure pandemonium. The disciples felt both helpless and hopeless. I can imagine the disciples thinking, "We are going to die! Our families will never see us again! We will never see land again and there is nothing we can do about it! Our lives are over!"Interestingly, not one time did the disciples consider the great power of their master; rather, they questioned Jesus, "Why are you letting this happen? Do you not care that we are perishing?"

Of course, the story ended in victory. Jesus, the hero of the day, commanded peace and for the wind to be still, and guess what, the winds obeyed. Although turmoil may come with your waiting room experiences, you, too, can command peace. All you have to do is learn to be still.

Say with me: When the situations of life cannot be controlled, God help me to be still and know that it is you who holds my tomorrow.

DAY 11:

THE MASTER PLAN

"For I know the plans I have for you," declares the LORD, "plans to prosper you and not to harm you, plans to give you hope and a future."

Jeremiah 29: 11

Before the waiting room of COVID-19 ever arrived, God already had a plan for each of us, a plan that you've probably not yet imagined. However, waiting room experiences are perceived as times of great discomfort. Therefore, when we encounter unpleasant experiences or experiences foreign to our day to day existence, we're quickly thinking of the best escape route possible.

In the Old Testament, there was a man by the name of Job. The writer describes Job as one possessing a high moral character: one who feared God and one who turned away from evil. Job was a very wealthy man, owning a big farm, abundant with animals. He had a beautiful wife and several children who were richly blessed because of him. Suddenly, the enemy of Job's soul was given permission, by God, to curse all that Job had. Job's cattle were abruptly taken away from him his servants and children were killed. What a waiting room of agony! I cannot imagine the suffering and the mental anguish that Job must have felt.

Interestingly, Job did not waiver in his faith toward God even with his wife begging him to curse God and die. Job's wife could not understand how was it that an all-powerful, all-knowing God would allow such a tragedy to destroy everything that she and Job had. Job's tragedy did not end there. The enemy came back and afflicted Job's physical body with countless sores, but Job stood firm in his belief in God. Despite his tragic waiting room experience, Job refused to curse his God.

Just like Job, you may experience a tragic waiting room of immense suffering through no fault of your own, but will you stand in faith like Job did, trusting that God still has a greater plan for your life? Job's life ended in great victory. The story recounts that Job was supremely blessed with twice as many riches than what he possessed before entering his tragic waiting room experience. He was also blessed with more children and his daughters were described as the most beautiful throughout the land. What a bonus!

I believe somewhere in Job's heart he knew that God's master plan was awaiting his arrival. Never forget that the master plan will not always come how you think it should. Just trust God in the process.

Say with me: God's plan for my life is bigger and better than I have ever imagined.

DAY 12:

SPEAK LIFE

"Death and life are in the power of the tongue."

Proverbs 18: 21

I've lived long enough now to understand that words have power. Words can heal, hurt, and destroy. In fact, numerous psychologists believe that a single word has the power to influence the expression of genes that control physical and emotional stress. Considering this information as plausible, let's both question and reason together: Why is it that so many people utter words that have the ability to taint their reality, make them feel ill, or blind their judgment?

Perhaps, the answer lies in our human DNA, our cultural backgrounds, and/or our plethora of life experiences.

One of my favorite Old Testament biblical stories recounts a challenging, yet liberating, waiting room experience of four leprous men. Because of their condition, they were banned from entering the city. In addition, they could not interact with other citizens of their culture or participate in any social events. Their situation was no different from the many people today who have been diagnosed with COVID-19. Once an individual tests positive with this tragic disease, he or she is required to enter a state of extreme separation from both family and society. In the 21st century, we call it quarantine.

A major turning point for the leprous men is when they ask the question amongst themselves, "Why should we sit here until we die?" In their current state, they would die from starvation and in the city that they were planning to enter, due to famine that had taken over the city; they would die there as well. I believe their question gave life to their unfortunate situation. Not only that, their question gave them the courage to get up and head toward the city on a quest to survive.

Imagine what would have happened to the four lepers had they said, "We might as well sit here because we're going to die anyway. There is no hope. This is our condition, and we have to accept it as it is." NO! They spoke life. The lepers' story ended well. They entered the Aramean camp, but no one was there. They entered the various tents, ate, and took many of the valuables and possessions that they had come across. What a story! You may have experienced some type of loss due to COVID-19, but guess what, you can still speak life. Speaking life despite your condition produces unexpected miracles. Therefore, I encourage you to never stop speaking life to your situation.

Say with me: I am looking forward to my miracle despite this waiting room experience.

DAY 13:

BEAUTY

"The heavens declare the glory of God; the skies proclaim the work of his hands."

Proverbs 19: 1

A few days ago, as I was walking through my neighborhood, I encountered my next-door neighbor. Interestingly, I've been living in my current neighborhood for two years, and this particular neighbor and I have never spoken to each other. Nevertheless, we introduced ourselves to each other and began to discuss briefly how COVID-19 had impacted our personal and professional lives and the world at large. What I found fascinating about our conversation is when my neighbor expressed, "I am thankful for the pandemic in a sense, because I now have a deeper appreciation for nature. I was just taking a walk in a park nearby, and I was thinking to myself how everything is just so beautiful."

Even in the worst of times, I find it amazing that we can still see God's beauty revealed in nature. Think about the sweet rays of the sunlight that light the day skies and the amazing stars that light the night skies. Think about the red robin that flies and perhaps lands on your mailbox and disappears within seconds. Think about the eclectic designs of the various types of trees in your back yard or a local park, or the gushing and gentle sounds of a lake nearby, or perhaps an unexpected rainbow after a storm has passed over.

Even in the waiting room, think about the beautiful things that you've encountered. How has God's beauty refreshed your soul lately?

Say with me: Thank you, God, for allowing me to see your beauty even in the most trying of times.

DAY 14:

FEARLESS

"When I am afraid, I put my trust in you."

Psalm 56: 3

Fear is probably one of the most daunting human emotions. We fear because we're afraid of the unknown. We fear because we are not in control. We fear because the dreams, the visions, and the aspirations that we thought were once possible have all of a sudden become impossible, and we fear because of words such as: "what if,""maybe,""I don't know," and the list goes on. Meanwhile, as COVID-19 has invaded our human experience, many of us have become consumed with fear. Many are thinking, "How will I meet my financial obligations? What about my job? (Lord knows I have to work). What about my children's education? How will I keep my business afloat, and will I have to exhaust my savings in order to survive?" Simply, fear has caused many to doubt this world's promised systems, themselves, and perhaps the very existence of God's presence.

Daniel is probably one of my favorite biblical characters. He was a praying man. In fact, he prayed three times a day, ensuring that he would not lose his connection with his God. Daniel was one character that refused to serve or acknowledge any other gods. One day, however, Daniel's faith was tested. There was a decree made throughout the land, ordering every person to make prayers only to the King's god. Daniel was fearless. He retreated to his prayer closet and continued to pray to the God of Israel. What a bold move, knowing that violation of the King's order would result in a horrible death. Can you imagine being thrown into a pit with a pack of hungry lions? Because Daniel refused to obey the King's order, he was thrown into a lion's den. Miraculously, God shut the mouth of every lion, and Daniel was released from the pit more victorious than ever.

I am sure Daniel was afraid. He was human just like you and I, but Daniel refused to let fear overtake him. His constant connection with God through prayer caused him to be a fearless warrior.

Don't let fear kill you in the waiting room.

Say with me: I command fear to die at its root. God is with me. Therefore, fear has no place in my life.

DAY 15:

HIGHER

Many are the plans in a person's heart, but it is the Lord's purpose that prevails."

Proverbs 19: 21

I shall never forget it. In the year 2010, I was abruptly terminated from my job. It was a horrible feeling. What made that firing so perplexing was that the company had recently promoted me and weeks later, I was let go. My immediate supervisor called me into her office and said, "You can no longer serve in this position." My heart dropped. "They are letting me go," I said to myself. More than that, I was given no concrete reason for my firing. Mind you, the promotion had allowed me to upgrade a few things in my personal life. I had moved into a bigger apartment and had recently purchased a new car. Now, my financial world had suddenly crashed. How would I support myself? Who would I call? Who could I lean on?

I wanted to throw a pity party, but the Spirit within me would not allow it. I filed for unemployment. As I collected weekly unemployment benefits, I decided to begin my own business. Within one year, my business began to grow, and yes, it was a deep struggle trying to keep the business afloat. However, things got better (as they always will). The business grew. I hired staff. Profits became a reality, and the list goes on . . .

When I look back on that awful experience of being fired, it was humiliating, trying to sneak out the office in order to escape the embarrassment of it all. I was in a waiting room of public shame coupled with feelings of recurring despair. God had blessed me, and all of a sudden, the blessing was abruptly taken away. I have now come to understand that many of the waiting room experiences that we encounter have been designed to take us higher.

Say with me: The sum of every experience, good or bad, has been designed to take me higher!

DAY 16:

SURGERY

"And I will give you a new heart, and I will put a new Spirit in you, I will take your stony stubborn heart and give you a tender, responsive heart."

Ezekiel 36:26

The idea of surgery on any part of the human body can be a frightening thought. Imagine having to be placed under anesthesia, and the doctors telling your family that it's a possibility you might not survive. You agree, however, with the surgical procedure because you believe that it is in the process of surgery that you will be healed or whatever is broken will be fixed.

Since COVID-19, I have encountered countless people and friends alike who have explained to me that the quarantine life feels like a major surgery. One individual told me, "You know, this is meant to be, I feel, like God is doing something new in my heart; I've been reflecting a lot lately." Another individual explained, "I feel like I am starting to think about life a little differently now." I've also been told, "Yeah, I don't like the inconvenience of this, not having to go to work and all, but I know God is working on me and I am coming out of this thing stronger than ever."

As you can see from each conversation, the waiting room experience is a difficult one. It snatches us out of our comfort zones, but we come to a realization that this is God's work. There's a quick realization, a revelation that God is actually changing my heart. I get it now; my spirit, my perspective, and my outlook are all being changed for the better.

You are currently experiencing a spiritual surgery. This divine surgery is necessary as you move into your next dimension of purpose and power!

Say with me: Prepare my heart, Oh God, for the greater life that you have for me. Anything that does not align with your plan for my life, please remove it.

DAY 17:

LOVE

"Give thanks to the God of heaven. God's love endures forever."

Psalm 136:26

I can tell you story after story of times when I felt unloved. Unfortunately, we don't get to choose the life we've been given. We have to deal with the hand we've been dealt. In fact, the other night, I asked God some serious questions concerning my own life. For example, why did my mother have me at age 16? Why did I have to repeat kindergarten? Why did I have to take speech therapy in the first grade? Why did I not meet my biological father until age 29? Why did I have to have my tonsils removed at an early age? Why was I told I would not graduate from high school? Why did I grow up in what many would call the 'hood? My waiting room experience has been full of recurring why(s).

Despite it all, I need you to understand that God's love lifts us all. God's love is lifting you, and God's love will continue to lift you. God's love is meeting you right where you are right now as you are reading this page. God's love comes without condition, and it is an everlasting love that cannot be explained. So, my waiting room experiences—though complicated—have not been so bad after all.

God's love has set me free.

Say with me: Thank you, Most High God, for loving without any conditions.

DAY 18:

PURPOSE

"I cry to God Most High, to God who fulfills his purpose for me."

Psalm 57:2

Since the inception of COVID-19, the lives of many have been severely impacted. I cannot visit the grocery store, scroll down my Facebook and Instagram pages, or watch the news without encountering some horrible and unfortunate report citing how COVID-19 has taken a toll on the lives of so many. In fact, I recently encountered a report about a doctor, here in the states, who committed suicide due to the great stress that she'd encountered in her attempt to combat COVID-19 amongst her patients. What a trage-dy! This virus has caused many to fall to their knees, giving up on God's greatest gift to humanity, the gift of life.

Last evening, Joe Biden, the current Democratic nominee for America's next presidential election, was asked a question at a town hall meeting: "Sir, being that you have lost a son and not long ago, what you would say to those who have lost loved ones due to COVID-19?" Biden re-sponded, "You have to learn to find your purpose when it's dark and let purpose guide you. In your purpose, you will understand that those loved ones are still here with you, and you will be able to help someone else with your story, but you have to find that purpose first."

Candidly, I was not expecting this novel type of re-sponse from Biden. I began to think ("WOW"); there is so much purpose in the most challenging of times. What a par-adox! Our purpose (divine, recurring destinations) allows us to push past the pain and see what God sees. This purpose is akin to an eagle soaring over the turbulent winds of life. Because the eagle's eyes are so fixed on its destination, those threatening winds become null and void. So, it is with you and me: getting lost in a purpose-driven life is a sure antidote for survival in times of crisis. To survive your waiting room experience, I encourage you to get acquainted with God's purpose for your life. Trust me, you have one and it's larger than life!

Say with me: My God-sized purpose is bigger than my present circumstance, and this purpose is leading me through the wait.

DAY 19:

FIGHT

"You come against me with sword and spear and javelin, but I come against you in the name of the Lord *Almighty."*

I Samuel 17: 45

There was biblical character by the name of David, who yelled out to a nine foot giant by the name of Goliath, "I come against you in the name of the Lord!" David's words indicated that there was a problem, and he was not willing to allow this enormous giant to defeat him, but how could David win victory over a giant so enormous in size, a giant filled with terror, and a giant that would demolish anything it its path? First, David was a very young shepherd boy, and second, David had no fighting skills or military background. Therefore, we can conclude from this angle of the story that David was preparing himself and Israel for a major defeat.

What I love about David is what many would see as impossible (a young boy bringing a giant to his knees), David saw as possible. David saw beyond the surface. He did not allow what he had heard about Goliath's terrorization of others stop him from standing toe-to-toe with this giant. David knew that the invisible God was already on the scene, warring on his behalf.

The waiting room is, oftentimes, filled with many giants, but you must be willing to fight. All you really have to do is move over to the sideline and let God fight the battle for you. Never forget that God has won every battle.

Say with me: I slay giants because the greater one, the Almighty God, fights for me each and every time giants appear.

DAY 20:

GRACE

"But he said to me, my grace is sufficient for you, for my power is made perfect in weakness. Therefore, I will boast all the more gladly about my weakness, so that Christ's power may rest in me."

2 Corinthians 12: 9

The year 2020 has seemingly come with a vengeance, and it is hard to understand the reasons why. First, the world was met with the unexpected death of our beloved Kobe Bryant, one of the great NBA legends of all time, his daughter, and several of his precious colleagues. Second, we experienced the fierce entry of a global pandemic called

COVID-19, resulting in thousands of deaths. Finally, there has been societal unrest, both nationally and globally, due to historic police brutality which has severely and disproportionately impacted the African American community. This waiting room experience is filled with tragedy, hurt, and pain, and it is a major challenge for many.

The Apostle Paul recounted how he had a thorn (weakness) in his life. Paul's thorn was so disturbing that he wanted it to be removed. His story is no different from what we are encountering today. We are pleading with God: "Please, oh God, make 2020 better! Invade our human experience, and bring about a radical change for the better. It feels as though you've taken a break from your throne. Where are you?" While these are legitimate questions, I believe God is responding to you and me just as he responded to Paul: "My grace is sufficient for you, despite the circumstance. In your troubles and uncertainties, I will strengthen you; and my grace, which is my power and goodwill toward you, will carry you through."

In this waiting room, you may be experiencing the loss of a loved one due to COVID-19 or some type of tragedy that I have not mentioned. I encourage you to expect God's provisions of grace to strengthen you in your weakest moments.

Say with me: God's grace has given me supernatural power to survive any situation, no matter how big or small.

DAY 21:

WORRY FREE

"Therefore I tell you, do not worry about your life, what you will eat or drink; or about your body, what you will wear. Is not life more than food and the body more than clothes? Look at the birds of the air; they do not sow or reap or store away in barns, and yet your heavenly feeds them."

Matthew 6: 25

To worry is a natural human emotion, but we must learn to not become consumed in our worry, especially in the waiting room. When I was a young boy, I found myself worried about getting new clothes for the start of every school year, until one day, my grandmother said to me, "Boy, you are going to worry yourself to death!" I took it literally and thought to myself, "If I keep worrying about these clothes, I am going to die!" But grandmother's message was conveying that too much worry can be detrimental to one's mind.

In your current waiting room experience, you must listen and obey the words of Jesus. He encouraged his followers not to worry about anything. The wait is filled with so much ambiguity and endless uncertainty, but your ability to not become consumed in worry is couched in your willingness to trust fully the words of Jesus. In fact, worrying is akin to a rocking chair, wavering back and forth over things that you cannot control.

Don't allow the waiting rooms of COVID-19 consume your mind with worry. If God takes care of the bird that you hear chirping, the lilies across the fields, and the animals in the ocean, surely, He will take care of you, His beloved creation.

Say with me: Worry no longer has any place in my life. Whatever the outcome of this waiting room experience is, I know that God will take care of me.

WAITING ROOM PRAYERS

Praying for Love

God, help me to love all people despite our differences. My job is to love as you have commanded me to love (I Corinthians 13: 4-7).

Praying for Peace

God, surround me with your everlasting peace. Let your peace consume my mind, body, and soul (I Peter 5: 7).

Praying for Protection

God, keep your hands of protection around me and my family. Protect every facet of our lives (Deuteronomy 31:6).

Praying for Guidance

God, lead me in every area of my life. Invade my human experience, and I will not fail at anything I put my hands to do (Jeremiah 42: 3).

Praying for Forgiveness

God, forgive me for anything that I have done both knowing and unknowingly. Help me to keep my heart and thoughts clean (I John 1: 19).

Praying for Others

God, I pray for every person who has been impacted by COVID-19. Strengthen their hearts and minds. Give them comfort and peace right where they are, and meet their every need (I Timothy 2: 1-5).

Made in the USA
Columbia, SC
14 December 2020

27894225R00041